Life in Inspiring Places

POEMS BY

CHERYL BATAVIA

INK START MEDIA
265 Eastchester Dr Ste 133 #102
High Point NC 27262

Life in Inspiring Places

POEMS BY

CHERYL BATAVIA

Dedicated with love
to my children,

Ellen, Joe, and Katey

Table of Contents

Preface 1

Acknowledgements 1

Perspectives 3

    Pencils 4

    Stars 5

    Behind the Scenes 6

    What a Great Day! 7

Favorite Places 9

    Let's Listen to Music! 10

    Blue Hole 11

    Shenandoah 12

    National Park 12

    Shenandoah Valley Vignettes 14

    DC 16

    Everglades 17

    Miami Beach 18

Florida Gulf Coast **21**

    Pelican Beach Party 22

    Netting in Lemon Bay 23

    Visiting Indian Mound 24

    Indian Mound on Lemon Bay 26

    In the Water at Last! 29

    A Return to the Beach 30

    Dolphins at Venice Jetty 32

    Solitude 33

Family **35**

    Brothers & Sisters 36

    Grandma 38

    Eat Watermelon! 40

    Watermelon 40

    Popcorn! 42

    Mockingbird Songs 43

    Soul Mate 43

    Clifford 45

Rites Of Passage **47**

    What's this World Coming to? 48

    Black-Eyed Susans 49

    Paper Dolls 50

    Work & Retirement 50

    Map Game 53

    Clouds 54

    Be Remembered Well 56

Photo Credits **57**

Preface

Life in Inspiring Places shares my memories and impressions of living in places surrounded by history and natural beauty. For nearly two decades, I lived in the picturesque Shenandoah Valley of Virginia. My oldest daughter grew up there, swimming and fishing in the Shenandoah River, hiking and picnicking in Shenandoah National Park, and visiting the historic sites of the Shenandoah Valley.

I played tourist for all of the ten years I lived in Washington, DC, enjoying festivals, exploring the city and the Smithsonian Museums, and attending a variety of performances at the Kennedy Center.

For the last quarter century, I have lived in Florida, a state with exquisite scenery and amazing biodiversity. My two younger children grew up in Miami Beach and Coconut Creek. We hung out at the beaches and in the Everglades and explored the state of Florida, learning about state history and the natural environment.

In 2011, I retired from teaching and moved to the Gulf Coast of Florida. Gulf beaches and nature preserves are on my doorstep. I lead a quiet, happy life, and I write poetry. I hope you enjoy this book, and I hope you are finding time to take delight in the beauty that surrounds you, wherever you are.

Cheryl Batavia

Acknowledgements

I would like to thank my sister Yolanda, whose critique of my writing has always been helpful to me. To my son Joe, who listened as I read my poems aloud and shared his perspectives, I appreciate you. Thank you to my daughters, Ellen and Katey, who said, "yes," when I asked for their help at book fairs. To Robert, who bought my books as gifts for his grandchildren, nieces and nephews, I will always be grateful for your support.

I would like to thank all of the people who provided encouragement and support in publishing this book, especially my advisor, Matthew Ross.

Thank you to Kem Enon, Romeo & Ink Start Media, book interior designer and book cover designer, for making this book beautiful.

Perspectives

Pencils

My long, black pencils
have short, black erasers…
I'm not always right.

Stars

Feeling small in the vastness
of a galaxy of stars,
I am comforted
by my own insignificance.
It doesn't matter very much
if I am rich or famous,
or even pure in heart…except to me.

I am free, with all the other
short-lived humans,
to simply enjoy this moment,
gazing at the stars,
finding inspiration for my
brief life, confident
that doing my best is enough,
feeling free to be happy!

Behind the Scenes

If I say I made my own luck, it may not be so.
Maybe someone helped me, and I didn't know.
When I fell on my face, I could have been
sabotaged by someone I thought was my friend.

Though I've tried to help my fellow man
and do good deeds whenever I can,
I know I've made enemies inadvertently,
and maybe helped others in ways I can't see.

I'm sure there were times that I was blind
to the needs of others; it weighs on my mind.
I'm sure I wasted energy trying to see
if somebody else was out to get me.

Life's about making the world a better place;
it's not about fighting to win the race
to the top of the ladder or to the bank,
or sacrificing integrity for power or rank.

I take compliments with a grain of salt,
and being blamed doesn't mean I'm at fault.
The opinions of others have merit, but…
it's sometimes best to go with your gut!

If I'm out there seeking a pat on the back,
It may be best to forget about that!
Accolades I receive may not be
the most reliable measure of my humanity.

What a Great Day!

It hadn't been the most exciting day,
so we decided to get away.
We should not have followed our hunch
to choose a fancy place for lunch.

The restaurant had been elegant before,
but they had "updated" to a tacky décor.
It was cold. We fidgeted in the hard chairs.
It was noisy, and we wished we weren't there.
When the food came, it was ordinary,
edible, but just barely.

It was nice outside, a warm, sunny day.
We got in our car and drove away.
Forget going out; we were glad to go home!
Lucky for us the day wasn't done…

In the sky were rosy clouds backlit by the sun,
above them, against the blue, a pale full moon.
As we drove home, the clouds faded to white,
and the full moon grew yellow and very bright.

We were awed by the sky, but there was more…
A colorful little box turtle met us at the door.
Another surprise! Our mood was transformed.
We completely forgot about being bored!

Favorite Places

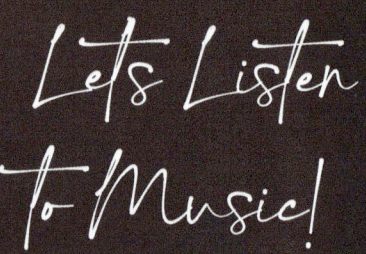

Let's Listen to Music!

I'll go with you to the symphony
to enjoy the harpist, horns, and timpani.
Will you walk on the beach at my side?
There's a concert by gulls and rushing tides.

I'd love to accompany you to the opera
and listen to the tenor and coloratura.
One day, let's visit the woodland clearing
to hear the arias mockingbirds are singing.

Sure! I'll hang out at the jazz club with you
and groove to piano, cello, and blues.
Will you stroll with me under starry skies,
as frogs and crickets improvise?

Blue Hole

Some Saturdays, after our chores were done,
we rushed to put our swimsuits on.
Dad carried the picnic basket to the car,
and we crossed mountains… It seemed so far!

Finally, we jumped into Blue Hole…
water clear as glass… and icy cold!
We watched couples sunning on rocks above,
necking and smooching; they were in love!

Dad got his fishing rod to catch some trout;
Mom ate tea berries and laid the picnic out…
homemade potato salad on my plate,
and the best hamburgers I ever ate!

Years later, I took my daughter to Blue Hole.
Our town swimming pool was never that cold!
She ate teaberries, as her grandma had done,
swam with the fish, and warmed up in the sun.

My brother and I were grown, not sure how old,
when he taught me to snorkel at Blue Hole.
For… maybe fifteen minutes… I followed the trout.
Then I heard, "It's been three hours! Let's get out!"
My brother showed the underwater world to me.
Blue Hole will always live in my memories.

11

Shenandoah National Park

There's no place like the Blue Ridge
to make me happy through and through,
mountains fading into the distance
in shades of green and blue.

There's no green like ferns
growing in drifts on the forest floor;
they make me feel alive
like I've never felt before.

No moment is quite like the
moment a deer appears with her fawn,
browsing at the edge of a meadow
in the hazy dawn.

There's nothing quite like
a waterfall to stir me in my soul,
flashing in the sunlight,
cascading to a shady pool.

No colors are quite like the reds and
yellows of maples in the fall.
The mountains are blazing with color,
and the morning air is chill.

Shenandoah winters are miracles
blanketed in white.
Icicles and snowy evergreens
glisten in the light.

Nothing signals springtime like the
green line, creeping up from valleys below,
bringing the mountains back to life
after the melting snow.

There's nothing more joyous than
wild flowers brightening the spring.
The trilliums and the mountain laurels
make my spirit sing.

There's nowhere like the Blue Ridge
to view the setting sun…
flaming colors soften… stars twinkle…
and lights in the valley come on.

Shenandoah Valley Vignettes

Shenandoah… famous in song and story,
the iconic Shenandoah River winds its way
northward through the legendary
Shenandoah Valley of Virginia.

Between the Blue Ridge Mountains on the
East and the Alleghenies on the West, lies the
valley, with its broad fields of corn and hay,
green pastures where cattle and horses graze,
apple orchards, vineyards, and poultry farms.

The historic Shenandoah County Courthouse,
the oldest courthouse west of the Blue Ridge,
still stands in Woodstock, Virginia.

At the Lutheran Church in Woodstock,
as the American Revolution began,
minister Peter Muhlenberg is said to have
removed his clerical robes one Sunday
morning, revealing a colonel's uniform.
He went on to a distinguished career
in the Continental Army and a successful
career in politics after the war.

In the northern Shenandoah Valley, you can
visit Harpers Ferry National Historical Park.
Here, the Shenandoah flows into the Potomac,
and here, John Brown made his famous raid.
He was apprehended by Robert E. Lee, who
later became head of the Confederate forces.

Rich in history, the Shenandoah Valley
is the site of numerous Civil War battles.
Known as "The Bread Basket of the South,"
the Shenandoah Valley was looted and burned
by General Sheridan's Union forces.

Edinburg women pleaded with
General Sheridan to spare the Edinburg Mill.
Union soldiers, who had set fire to the mill,
helped the townspeople put it out
with water from Stony Creek.
You can still see scorch marks in the mill.

In New Market, you can tour the battlefield
where very young Virginia Military Institute
cadets gave their lives for the Confederacy,
and visit the museum that tells their story.

Near the city of Harrisonburg, Amish
and Old Order Mennonites live on beautiful
farms and drive horse-drawn buggies.

There is a lot to do in the Shenandoah Valley:
Natural Bridge, the Apple Blossom Festival,
Belle Grove Plantation, museums, wineries,
caverns, historic inns, hiking, canoeing…

For nearly twenty years, I lived with my
family in the small town of Edinburg.
The Shenandoah Valley was our home…
and our playground.

My oldest daughter, Ellen, grew up there,
swimming and fishing in the Shenandoah
River, hiking and picnicking in
Shenandoah National Park.

After school, she loved to walk down the
mountain to the river, her cat Sunshine
by her side. She fed the birds in winter
and went sledding in the snow.

We visited many inspiring places in and around
the Shenandoah Valley while we lived there,
but I am sure there are a few we missed!

DC

Washington, DC has monuments,
fountains, flowers, and trees.
Smithsonian Museums overflow
with art, science, and history.

You can tour DC's historic landmarks
or observe the workings of government.
You can enjoy a cruise on the Potomac
or attend a Kennedy Center concert.

DC's restaurants and festivals
represent every culture, it seems.
In DC, you rub elbows with tourists and
immigrants chasing American Dreams.

I learned as much from ten years
of working and playing in DC
as I did from the degrees I earned
at two DC universities.

In a world of human imperfection,
DC's grandeur embodies equality,
justice, and liberty. Perfect ideas
surround us in Washington, DC.

Everglades

Do you remember the airboat rides
our family took in the Everglades?
We visited an island in the River of Grass
with a chickee hut and pet raccoons.
Do you remember the Miccosukee
Indian Village and the alligator shows?

Katey, you are no longer a little girl
holding a baby alligator in your hands.
Joe, you are no longer a little boy
sitting on the alligator's back
or shimmying up the greased pole
at the festival to win twenty dollars.

I hope you will always remember
those happy times in the Everglades
and all the other happy times you spent
with your father and me,
your grandparents, and our family.

Miami Beach

Sunshine on waves is an exciting show
for our daughter Katey and our son Joe.
Miami Beach is the perfect place to swim!
Mom and Dad keep an eye on them.

Zooming by slower folks is just great
for two little daredevils on roller skates!
It's the nineties. Skating is all the rage
for rollerbladers of every age.

The warm sea breezes are pure delight.
We're dining on Ocean Drive tonight.
Pizza and ice cream in a sidewalk café,
people passing in an endless parade.

Coming in, like a wave, is a happy mood.
We're listening to music and feeling good.
Mom and Dad still have dessert to eat.
Joe and Katey are dancing in the street!

Florida Gulf Coast

Pelican Beach Party

Young rascals were being foolhardy
when they tried to crash a pelican party.
Flapping their wings, the pelicans squawked,
"Hey Bud, it's time you walked!
Find your own sand bar, in a hurry!"

Netting in Lemon Bay

For several hours that morning, in blazing sun,
our group waded in the knee-deep muck
of Lemon Bay, netting sea creatures
and collecting them in pails. Then we gathered
on shore with the naturalist to observe and
discuss the animals we had found:
juvenile flounder, shrimp, tiny crabs…

I left a bit early because I had a lunch date
with a man who lived nearby.
We had been communicating on *Plenty of Fish*
and were meeting for the first time.
Woops! There were no showers at the park!
I cleaned up the best I could with a wet towel.

Still sweaty on top and muddy on the bottom,
I went to meet my date at Chili's.
We met in the parking lot with a hug
and a kiss on the cheek, not my usual handshake.
We talked for two hours over chicken fajitas.
Time flew by! I felt I had known him forever!
… That's how I met my soul mate!

Visiting Indian Mound

I heard about Indian Mound when
I went netting in Lemon Bay.
I had never seen an Indian mound,
and my curiosity was piqued.
"We'll go there," my new friend said.

We climbed the mound,
a tree-covered hill in a place
where hills are unexpected.
We sat on a bench overlooking
Lemon Bay and talked,
getting to know each other better.

We have returned to Indian Mound
many times over the years we've
been together. It is a great place
for conversation or contemplation!

I sit looking out over Lemon Bay
or wade along the muddy shore
and try to imagine the way of life
of the people who built the mound.

Indian Mound on Lemon Bay

Unearthing ancient garbage from
shell middens, we discover how people
lived in the far distant past. Shell middens
hide their secrets in layers, newest on top.
What's buried in this mound on Lemon Bay?
Clam and oyster shells, animal bones,
pottery shards, spear points, shell tools?

Paleo Indians came to the Florida Gulf Coast
more than twelve thousand years ago.
Some of them made their home on Lemon Bay.
The climate was drier then, and water levels in
Lemon Bay were lower. Large land mammals
inhabited Florida. Maybe mastodon bones
lie at the lowest level of this Indian mound!

Over millennia, climate changed, water levels
rose, and large land mammals disappeared.
Native Americans adapted to the changing
climate. Over time, various groups of
Native Americans lived here, each adding
their own layer of artifacts to Indian Mound.

The Calusahacthee were living on Lemon Bay
when Spanish explorers arrived in the 1500s.
Calusas, a powerful group with a complex
culture, were no match for European invaders.

What caused their decline? European diseases?
Superior European weapons? The Calusas were
gone about 200 years after Europeans arrived.
Remnants of the Calusa People are thought
to have joined the Seminoles.

A 7000-year-old burial ground,
twenty feet below the surface of Lemon
Bay,
was discovered in 2016.

Native Americans living here had wrapped
their dead in hand-woven cloth,
anchoring them to the bottoms of shallow
ponds with long, fire-hardened poles.

Over millennia, rising water covered
the ancient burial ground.
These human remains are protected by law,
destined to lie forever under Lemon Bay.

In the Water at Last!

Home… so close to the beach…
about half a mile as the osprey flies.
In the car, I share the beach road
with pedestrians and bicycles.

High on the drawbridge,
small boats anchored below,
sun sparkling on Lemon Bay and
the Gulf of Mexico beyond.

Parking lot overflowing with
snowbirds: West Virginia,
Michigan, Kentucky, Ontario…

Picnic tables shaded by
cabbage palms and sea grapes.
Yellow tickseed flowering
exuberantly in a patch of sunshine.

Hot, dry sand where umbrellas
bloom in multicolored splendor,
and a scent of coconut lingers.

Sunbathers lounge on blankets,
people-watching, chatting,
reading, eating potato chips.

Addicted granny in a beach chair
sneaks a smoke; holding my breath,
I move quickly beyond her!

I cross the high-water-mark, where
pastel shells and tiny black shark teeth
mingle… to the wet sand where castles
are slowly washing away, moat-first.

Young and old beachgoers stroll by,
showing off tattoos and suntans.
Shark tooth hunters scoop up the
wash with long-handled strainers.

Bikini-clad mom, ring in her navel,
dips the feet of her squealing baby
into the Gulf of Mexico.

In the water at last!
I wade through a school of minnows
and swim out to find
my own small piece of solitude.

A Return to the Beach

Karenia brevis… such a pretty name…
Such an ugly reality for the state of
Florida!
The stench of death wafting up from the
beach and seeping into our houses.
Months of red tide: cabin fever, coughing,
struggling to breathe, malaise.
Motels, restaurants, charter boat captains…
many businesses… all wondering
if the snowbirds will ever return…

Officially, the red tide has been over
for several months now, though toxic
blue-green algae still fouls our rivers.
Snowbird cars with license plates from
Ontario, Indiana, Vermont, Montana have
crowded beach parking lots all season long.
A plague of blizzards, northern
climate change, may bother snowbirds
more than Karenia brevis!

I have been recovering my strength.
Though the carnage is past, I am haunted
by the smell of dead fish. I grieve the loss
of sea turtles, manatees, and dolphins.
I must overcome my fears and sorrow…
walk on the sand, swim in the water.
Today is the day! I will return to the beach!

The sun is shining on pristine white sand,
a fresh breeze blows in over bright blue water.
A long, silvery shoal of tiny fish swim
just beyond the surf. A flock of pelicans
are having a party far out on the sand bar…
No humans allowed! I swim for a while,
then walk along the beach, enjoying the sun
and collecting shark teeth.

Marveling at Mother Nature's resilience,
I am filled with hope that Florida may recover.
The hurricanes that stir up sediments from
the floor of the Gulf and Lake Okeechobee
may be intensifying… climate change.
Is it a natural cycle beyond our control?

We do have the power to clean up
Lake Okeechobee, stop releasing runoff
into our rivers and oceans, and restore
the flow of water to the Everglades. We can
investigate issues of climate change, and
plan a future with a healthier environment.
We have the power. Do we have the vision?
Can we exercise the will?

Kudos to the State of Florida for renovating the dikes at Lake Okeechobee!

More water is now being released into the Everglades as nature intended, and less water is being released into rivers. Toxic algal blooms in Florida rivers and the Gulf of Mexico appear to be behind us.

Dolphins at Venice Jetty

We joined an excited jetty crowd,
"oohing" and "awing," but not too loud,
at a thrilling, all-star performance
wild dolphins were giving for us.

Jumping for joy, they put on a show
that lasted for fifteen minutes or so.
We were their chosen audience…
They liked us! I was touched.

I hope that I can always be
the friend the dolphins saw in me.

Solitude

Time for reflection…
a small space for solitude
brings me peace of mind.

Family

Brothers & Sisters

Mom didn't say I have to like you.
She said, "Be nice to each other."

Dad didn't say I have to like you.
He said, "Share your toys."

Grandma didn't say I have to like you.
She said, "Take turns."

Grandpa didn't say I have to like you.
He said, "Keep your hands to yourself."

Nobody said I have to like you…
but I do!

Grandma

Our Grandma, Frances Ellen Tustin, had to
babysit, so she left after two years of school.
She had learned to read! She used that skill
to educate herself and lived her life to the full.

At twelve, Grandma worked as a hotel maid.
Married at seventeen, she had two sons.
She and Grandpa worked hard to support
their family during the Great Depression.

Our grandparents moved a lot, flipping houses.
Grandma wallpapered, painted, and plastered.
The last house they renovated was her childhood
home, using all the skills they had mastered.

Grandma lived there for more than thirty years,
raising chickens, planting grapes and fruit trees.
She grew asparagus, strawberries, and flowers,
and cultivated her garden into her eighties.

Grandma decorated her home with hooked rugs,
handmade quilts, and afghans she crocheted.
Her grandchildren were always proud
to wear the beautiful clothes she made.

Cooking in restaurants and caring for the sick…
Grandma had many jobs over the years.
She was a long-time Sunday school teacher
who had earned the respect of her peers.

We always ate well at Grandma's house…
Everybody loved her black walnut cinnamon buns!
Grandma fed us chicken cacciatore and cookies.
We gathered eggs in the henhouse. That was fun!

In summer, Grandma gave strawberries to
friends and neighbors and made strawberry pies.

A huge bowl of strawberries waited for us at
Grandma's. We couldn't eat them all, but we tried!

The Raggedy Ann and Andy dolls Grandma made
were in demand at local gift shops.
The dolls she made for her great grandchildren,
were always loved a lot!

Most of my generation wanted to be like Grandma.
Great granddaughters, and great nieces, too,
are named "Frances" or "Ellen," or "Tustin," a gentle
reminder: Be known by the good works you do.

39

Eat Watermelon!

Buy a watermelon
off the back of the truck,
and don't forget to thump it!

Cool it in the creek
while we fish and swim…
Plenty for everybody!

Hey, you guys!
I bet you can't spit seeds
as far as I can!

Eat watermelon
as it dribbles off your chin,
Eat watermelon… and grin.

Watermelon

Watermelon… sweet!
Red and green and icy cold.
Hurry up… Cut it!

Popcorn!

When you were a kid, Mom,
did Nana make you popcorn
when you watched videos?

Would it be okay
to give Zelda some popcorn?
I think she's tired of baby food!

Mom! Cleopatra won't eat
her popcorn. Why?
Rufus likes it!

Mom, why does Rufus fart
when he eats popcorn?
… Sorry I said, "fart"!

Some popcorn didn't pop.
Could we plant it in the yard?
Why not?

Why does popcorn pop?
If you don't know the answer,
don't worry, Mom.
Just pop more popcorn! Please.

Mockingbird Songs

Home is mockingbird songs,
bees on bright flowers,
armadillos and bobcats
as neighbors.

Home is the company
of the one I love,
who understands me,
and loves me as I am.

Wherever I go, my thoughts
soon return home
to mockingbird songs…
and the one I love.

Soul Mate

Making love, or soup,
or conversation with you…
always my soul mate.

Clifford

Clifford, you were a joyful presence in our lives!
The day I brought you home, an abandoned
six-pound puppy in a cardboard box,
the two children met us at the door, shouting,
"Clifford! Clifford!" and that was your name.
Fortunately, you never grew to such enormous
proportions as Clifford, the Big Red Dog!

For fourteen years, you made us laugh and
comforted us when we were sad. You protected us,
looked out for us, and played with us.
Everyone loved you. The day Dad died, you slept
with the kids and me in the king-sized bed,
and every night after that, you slept at the foot
of my bed. Thank you for being there!

Every evening when I came home from work,
you met me at the door, tail wagging and all four
feet off the floor. Your enthusiasm was contagious!
You accompanied the children on their adventures.
I always knew they were safe with you.

The children grew up. When they came home
for a visit, it was like they had never left…
You always belonged to each other!
Thank you, Clifford, for being in our lives.

Rites Of Passage

What's this World Coming To?

Costs today are skyrocketing.
Look how much the plumber is pocketing!

Technology is changing way too fast!
Let's continue doing things as we did in the past.

Singers today sound like sick cats!
And why do parents let kids dress like that?

Nothing these days is made to last.
Quality and service are things of the past!

You won't hear me making remarks like this;
I may be over the hill, but I try to resist!
Well, you might hear me say a thing or two,
but only when I am sure that it's true!

Black-Eyed Susans

Black-eyed susans, growing around
a little country church in Pennsylvania,
caught the fancy of a five-year-old,
who took them home to Sunday dinner.

Black-eyed susans, growing on the bank
of a favorite swimming hole in Virginia,
caught the fancy of a young man,
who brought them home to his wife.

Black-eyed susans at the garden center,
too fancy and refined to tempt
the middle-aged gardener, but close enough
to stir the memory of something wild and free.

Black-eyed susans in a Florida supermarket
(sunflowers, but close enough)
caught the fancy of an older woman,
who brought them home to make her smile.

Paper Dolls

Under the full moon,
two shadows walk hand-in-hand...
giant paper dolls.

Work & Retirement

I don't set a clock, and that's no loss!
I'm seldom idle, but I'm my own boss.
When I look back over my life, I can see
how important work has been to me.

Work supports you and your family
and helps to shape your identity.
I had many jobs; I learned from every one,
but teaching was my true vocation.

I wanted to give students the world, but I see
that students gave the world to me.
I learned with them and from them every day.
"Learning is Fun!" as our sign used to say.

Map Game

Okay class, it's time to play the map game!
How many continents can you name?
Work together, and win points for your team…
What is the capital of the Philippines?
A long river in Egypt, a large Russian Lake,
A mountain range in the eastern United States,
A canal that links Atlantic and Pacific Oceans…
Great job, class! Hope you all had fun.

Clouds

Nearly ninety, Mom still liked to come
to Sunday dinner at our home.
After dinner, we'd watch an old movie,
Mom's cat Kitzey stretched out by her knee.
We'd call up relatives and have a chat,
as she sat stroking her purring cat.
Our dog Clifford wanted petting, too…
That was something Mom was happy to do.

Mom always enjoyed long country drives.
She would smile, her eyes coming alive,
watching egrets and cranes or horses and cows,
but most of all, she loved looking at clouds.
"Those clouds look like a fawn and a deer.
That one's a man with a long, white beard."

She never grew tired of seeing the sky of blue
and clouds with sunlight shining through.
I think she imagined Heaven to be in that space,
and she was going soon to that wonderful place.
"Isn't it beautiful?" she'd always say,
and knowing she was happy made my day.

When we were kids, Mom shared the charms
of an idyllic childhood on her family's farm.
Now, the farmers market was our place to go
to buy carrots to feed the horses and goats.
Mom visited the peacocks, roosters and hens,
pigs in the barn, and rabbits in their pens.

We bought pumpkins and chrysanthemums,
horehound, lemon drops, and Teaberry Gum,
but no trip to the market would be complete
without an ice cream cone for a treat.
So many flavors, Mom could always find
a flavor that was one of her favorite kinds!

Mom loved her family, and nearly every day,
we talked about family members far away.
One day I visited Mom; she was resting in bed.
"You've been a good daughter to me," she said.

Though home was now an independent living,
she was still my mom, still caring and giving.
For her, things were not how they used to be,
but she always took an interest in me.

Be Remembered Well

To be remembered well,
live well. Do praiseworthy deeds
in your time on earth.

Sea-beach-ocean-tropical-paradise- from **Pixabay**

Photo of Cheryl Batavia by **Katey Batavia**

Aerial View of the Town of Harpers Ferry, West Virginia...

located between the Potomac River and the Shenandoah

River by **sframe**

Doyles River Falls (in Shenandoah National Park) by **Paul Lemke**

Milky Way by **Manuel**

Looking up into a Maple in Full Fall Colors by **wilderpix**

African American Saxophonist, Sax Jazz Music by **Geoff Goldstein**

Blue Hole on Naked Creek, Rockingham County, Virginia

by **Taber Andrew Bain, CCBY2 0**

Rainbow trout by **Jeremy Pawlowski**

White-tailed Deer Fawn by **Paul**

Rolling Clouds over the Blue Ridge Mountains by **Cole**

Fall Colors at Shenandoah National Park by **Michael**

Mountain Laurel in Meadow and View of Old Rag by **jonbilous**

Washington, DC Monuments at Night under Full Super Moon by **Eric**

Miami, South Beach Sunset, Ocean Drive by **lunamarina**

Live Oak, Resurrection Fern, and Saw Palmettos by **Funderburke Photos**

A Brown Pelican in the Gulf of Mexico, Florida by **Norm**

Motorboat Pleasure Cruise by **Wimbledon**

Great Egret and Black-necked Stilt by **Luis Santos**

Children on the Beach by **Marzanna Syncerz**

Father and Son Playing in the Sea by **Max Topchil**

Group of Jumping Dolphins, Beautiful Seascape and Blue Sky by **Muratart**

Nature...Mangroves at Everglades National Park... by **littleny**

Miami Beach Palms by **ellensmile**

Brother and Sister Back to Back by **WavebreakmediaMicro**

Grandparents with Grandchildren in Pool by **aletia2011**

Fresh Watermelon by **Christian Jung**

Friend to Watch Sunset with Me (Florida Bobcat) by **Don Miller, CCBY2 0**

Beautiful Labrador Retriever... by **paola maria airenti**

Crystal River in Florida (Manatee)...by **Janos**

Gloriosa Daisy Indian Summer by **nahhan**

Lady's Slipper Orchid by **ChrWeiss**

Studying Geography by **pressmaster**

Clouds in Blue Sky by **wuttichai**

Red Columbine Flower Growing in a Forest with Mossy
Wood and Ferns by **holly**

*Photos are from Adobe Stock Photos except where noted otherwise.

www.ingramcontent.com/pod-product-compliance
Lightning Source LLC
Chambersburg PA
CBHW041520120626
46551CB00018B/2511